Color By Number Adult Coloring Book of Winter Birds

This Winter Birds Coloring Book belongs to:

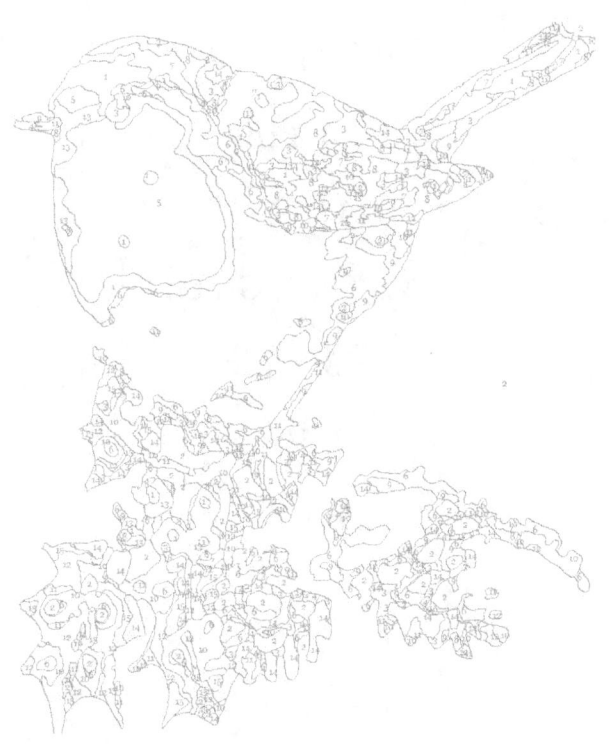

Copyright © 2018 Winter Birds Coloring Books

1. Black
2. Green
3. Blue
4. Brown
5. Purple
6. Light Blue
7. Light Green
8. Orange
9. Dark Red
10. Pink
11. Red
12. Dark Green
13. Gold
14. Violet
15. Yellow

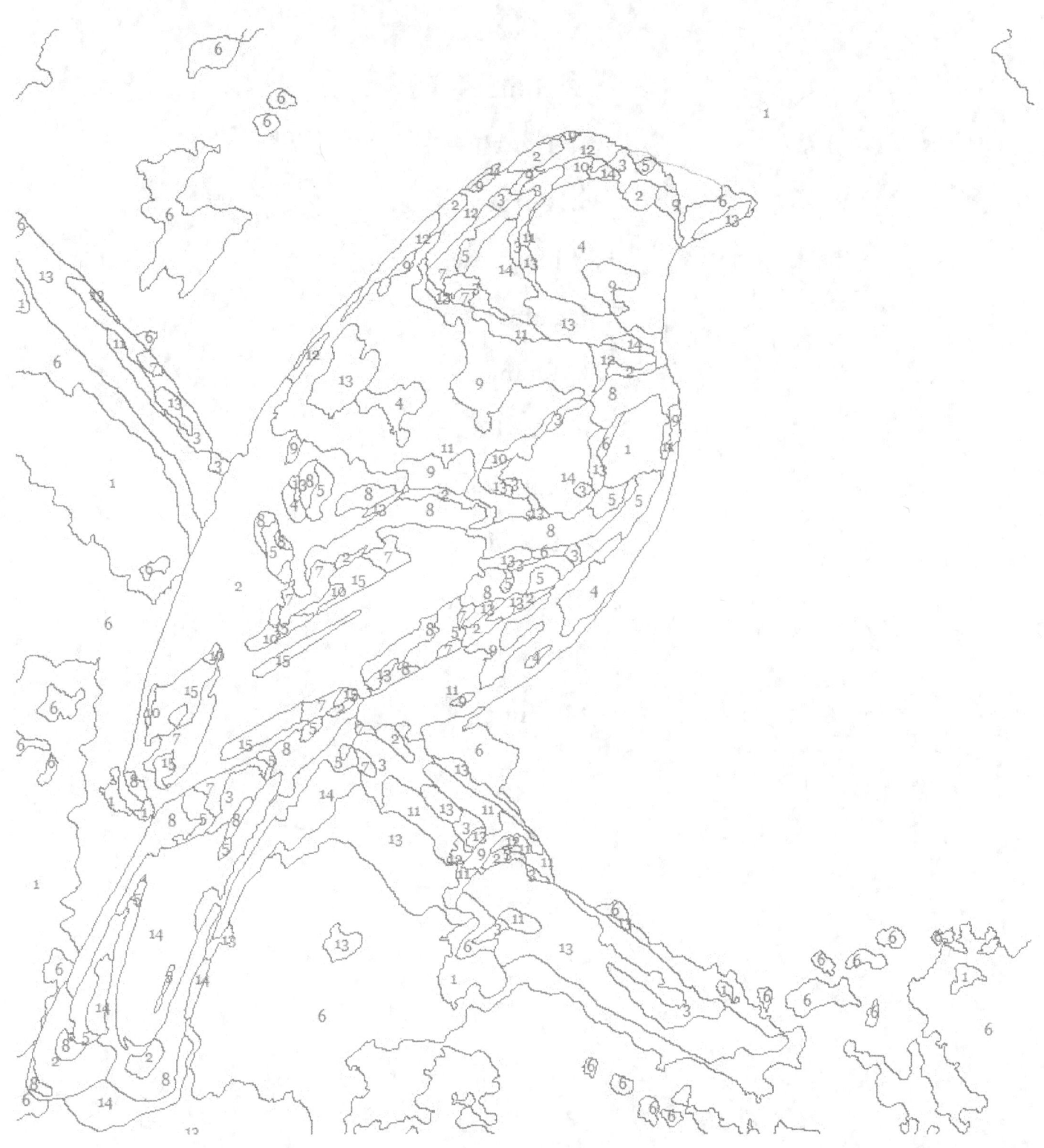

1. Black
2. Green
3. Blue
4. Brown
5. Purple
6. Light Blue
7. Light Green
8. Orange
9. Dark Red
10. Pink
11. Red
12. Dark Green
13. Gold
14. Violet
15. Yellow

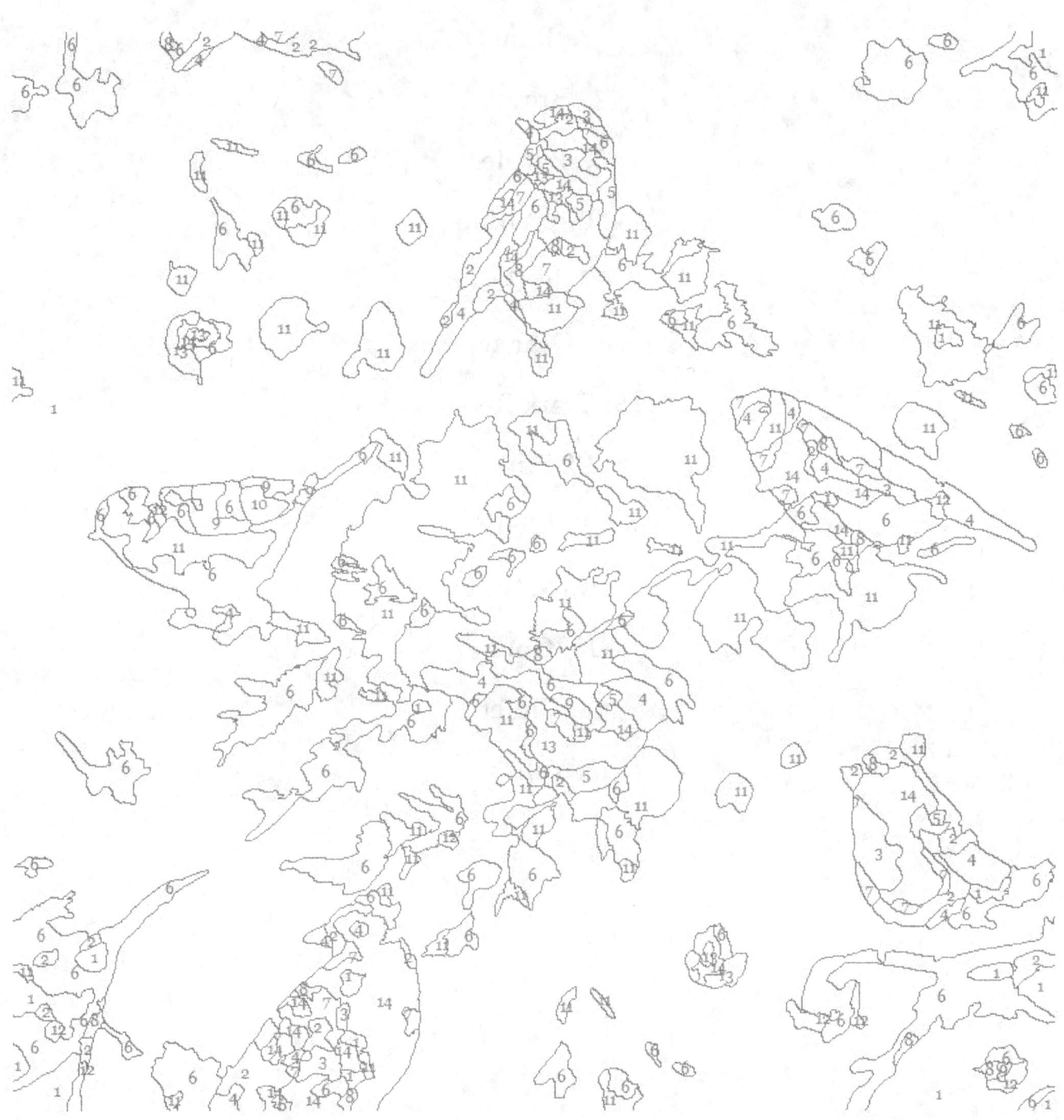

1. Black
2. Green
3. Blue
4. Brown
5. Purple
6. Light Blue
7. Light Green
8. Orange
9. Dark Red
10. Pink
11. Red
12. Dark Green
13. Gold
14. Violet
15. Yellow

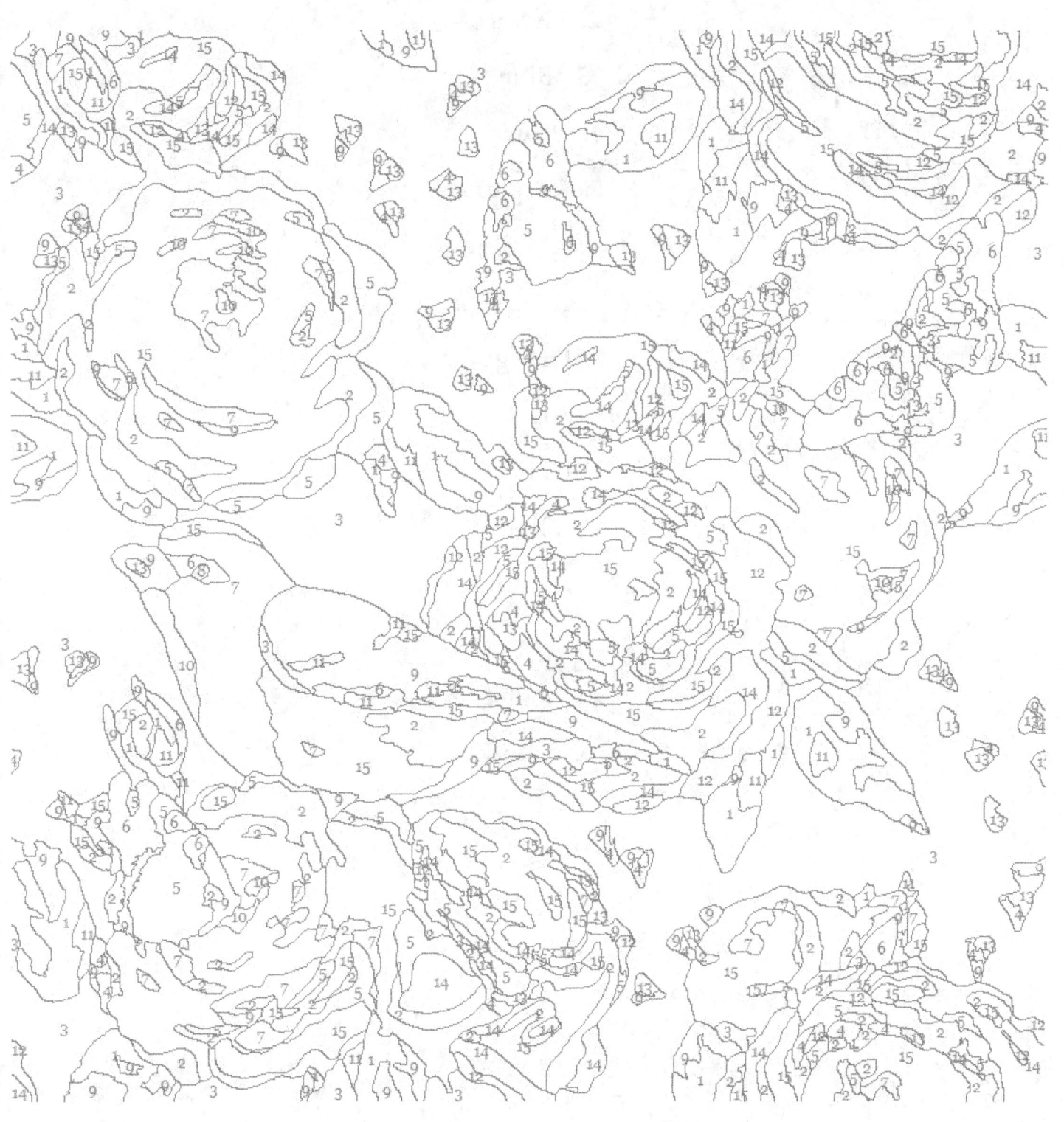

1. Black
2. Green
3. Blue
4. Brown
5. Purple
6. Light Blue
7. Light Green
8. Orange
9. Dark Red
10. Pink
11. Red
12. Dark Green
13. Gold
14. Violet
15. Yellow

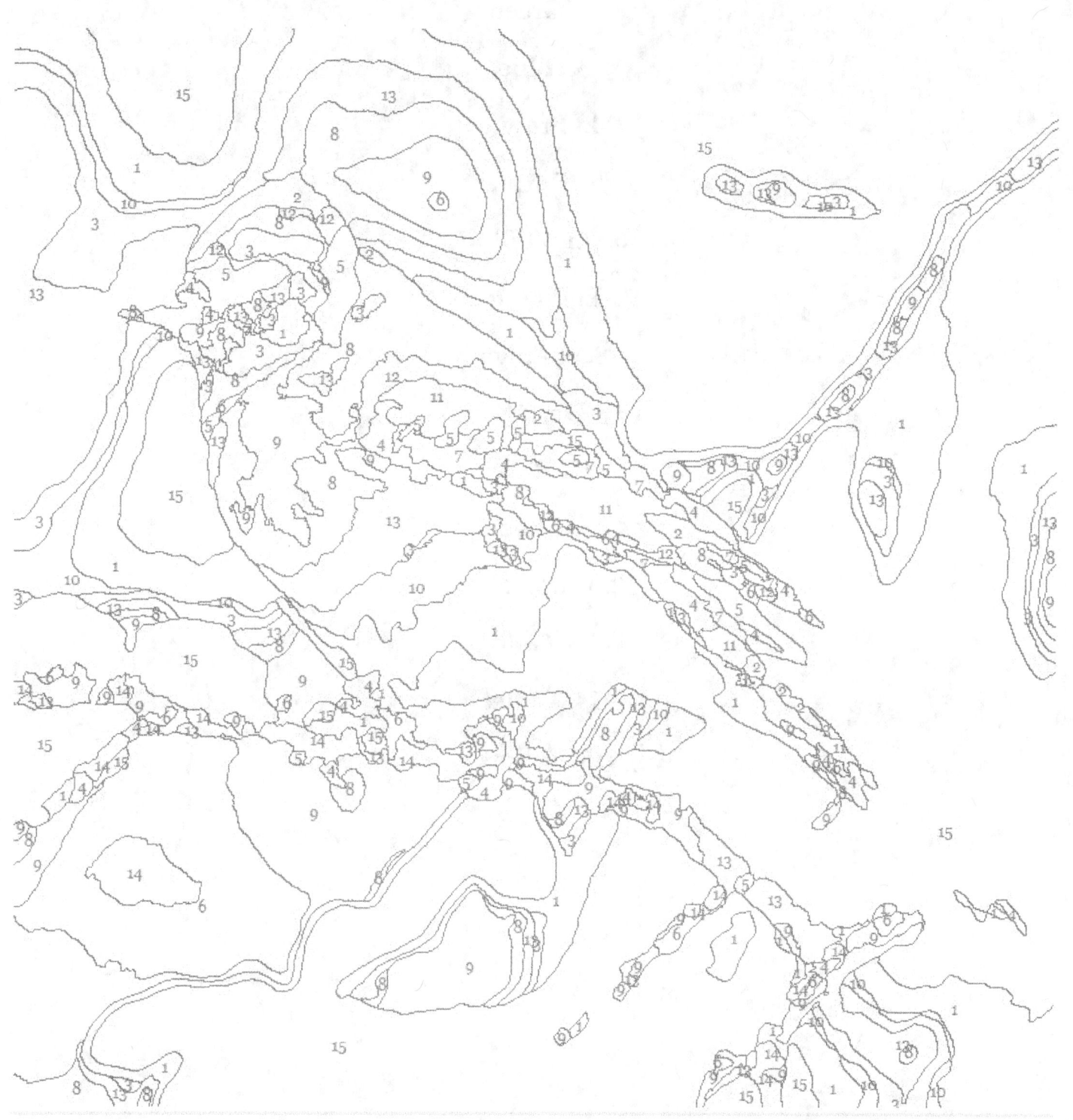

1. Black
2. Green
3. Blue
4. Brown
5. Purple
6. Light Blue
7. Light Green
8. Orange
9. Dark Red
10. Pink
11. Red
12. Dark Green
13. Gold
14. Violet
15. Yellow

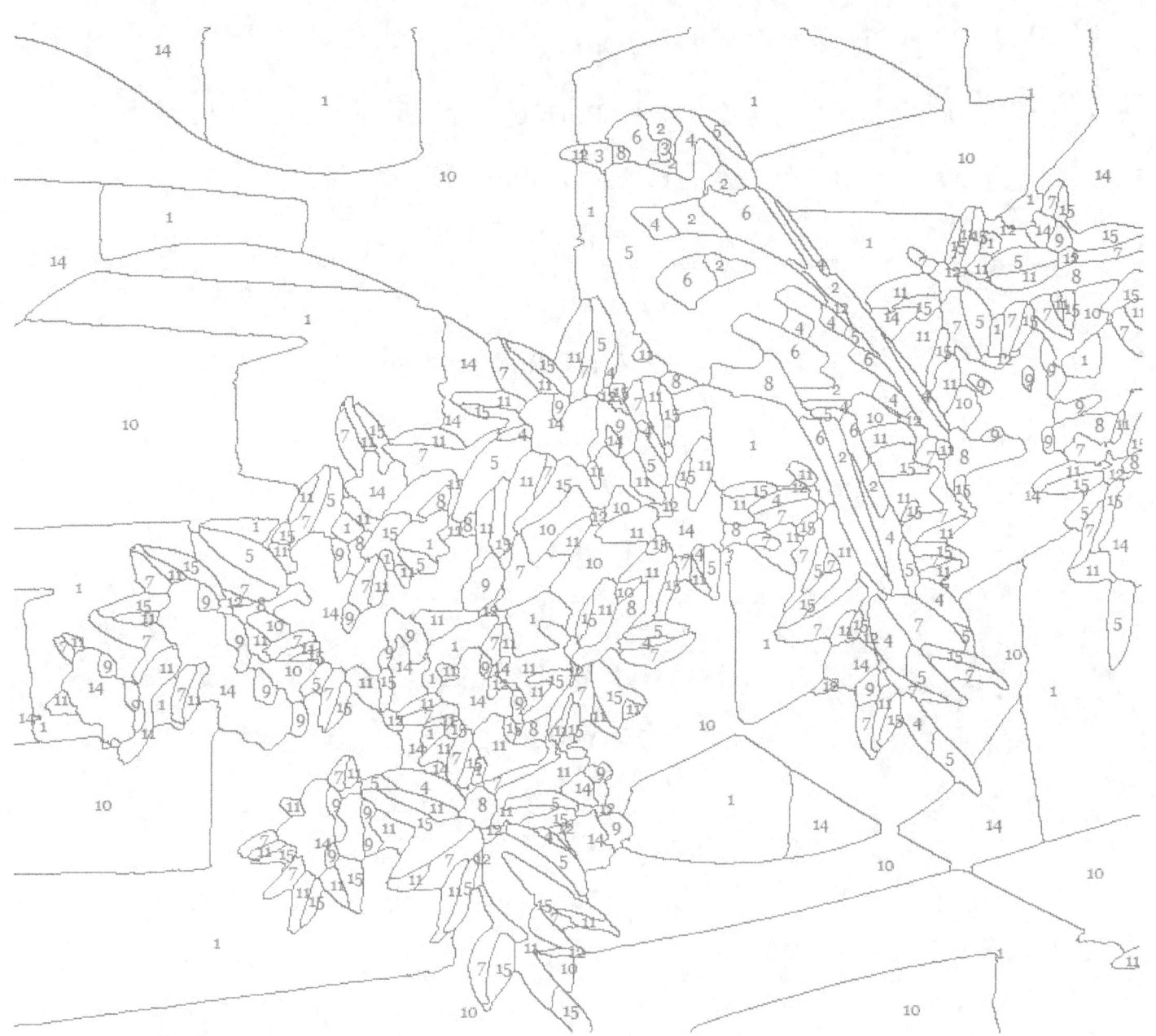

1. Black
2. Green
3. Blue
4. Brown
5. Purple
6. Light Blue
7. Light Green
8. Orange
9. Dark Red
10. Pink
11. Red
12. Dark Green
13. Gold
14. Violet
15. Yellow

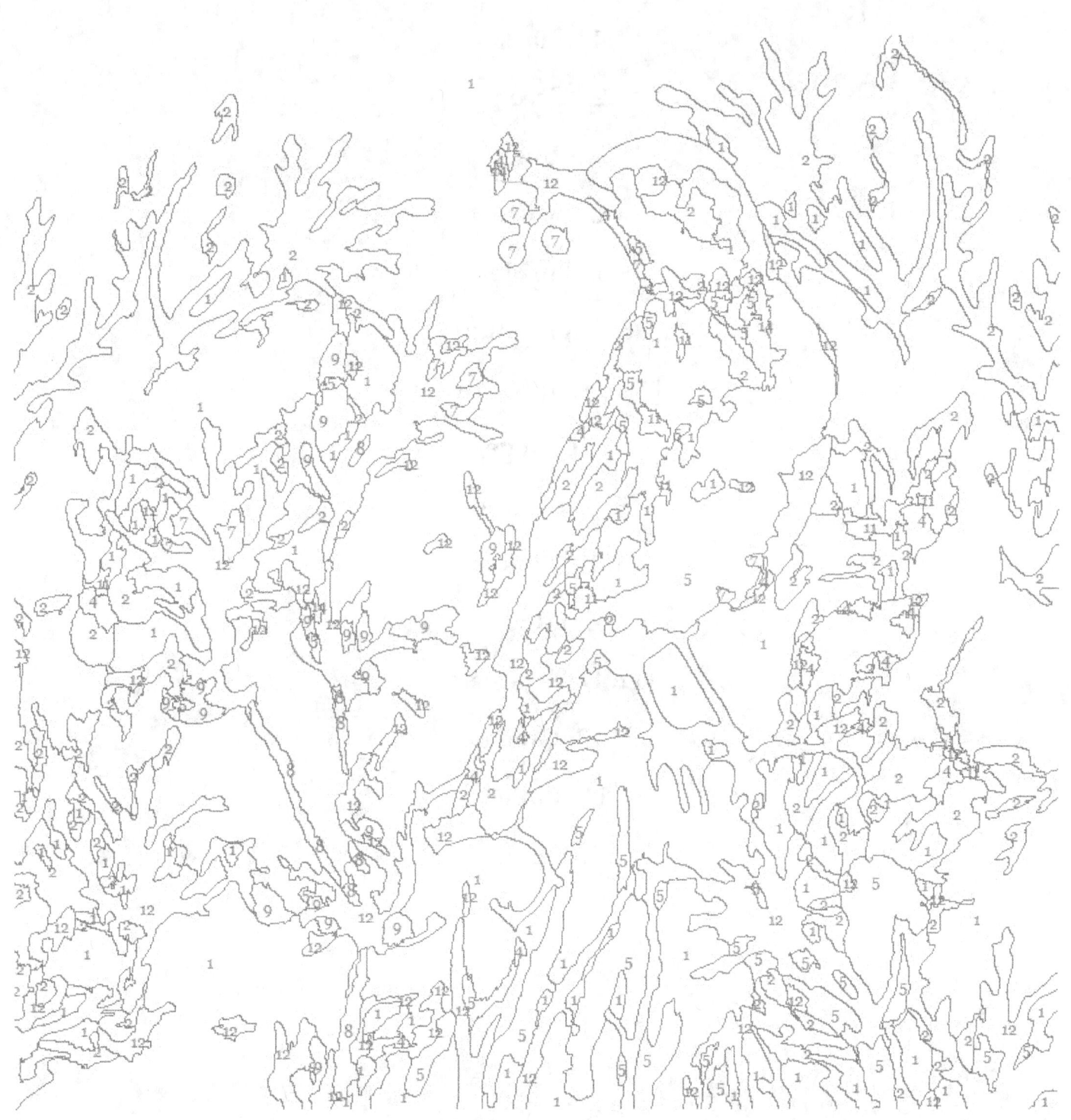

1. Black
2. Green
3. Blue
4. Brown
5. Purple
6. Light Blue
7. Light Green
8. Orange
9. Dark Red
10. Pink
11. Red
12. Dark Green
13. Gold
14. Violet
15. Yellow

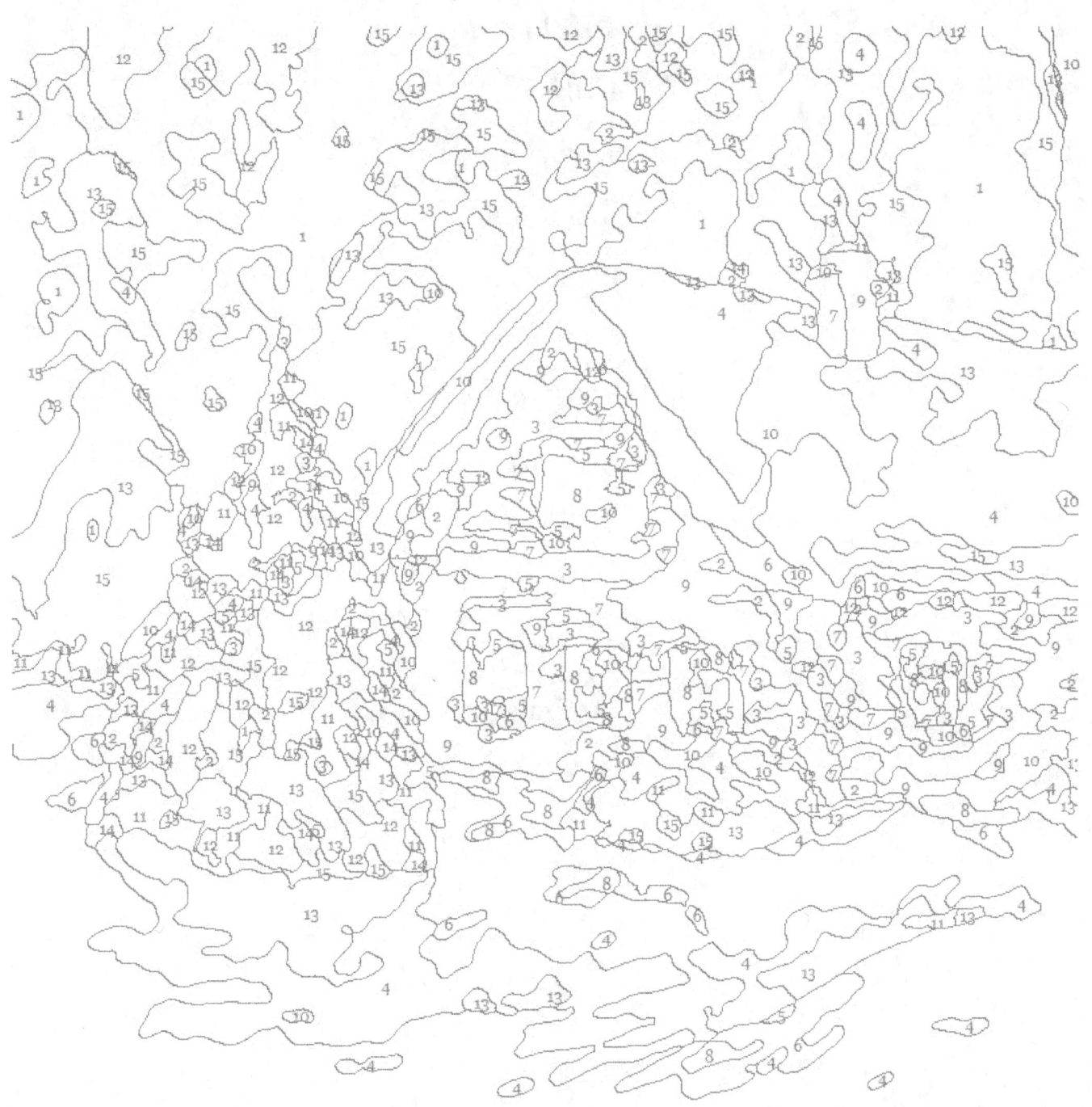

1. Red
2. Green
3. Blue
4. Brown
5. Purple
6. Light Blue
7. Light Green
8. Orange
9. Dark Red
10. Pink
11. Black
12. Dark Green
13. Gold
14. Violet
15. Yellow

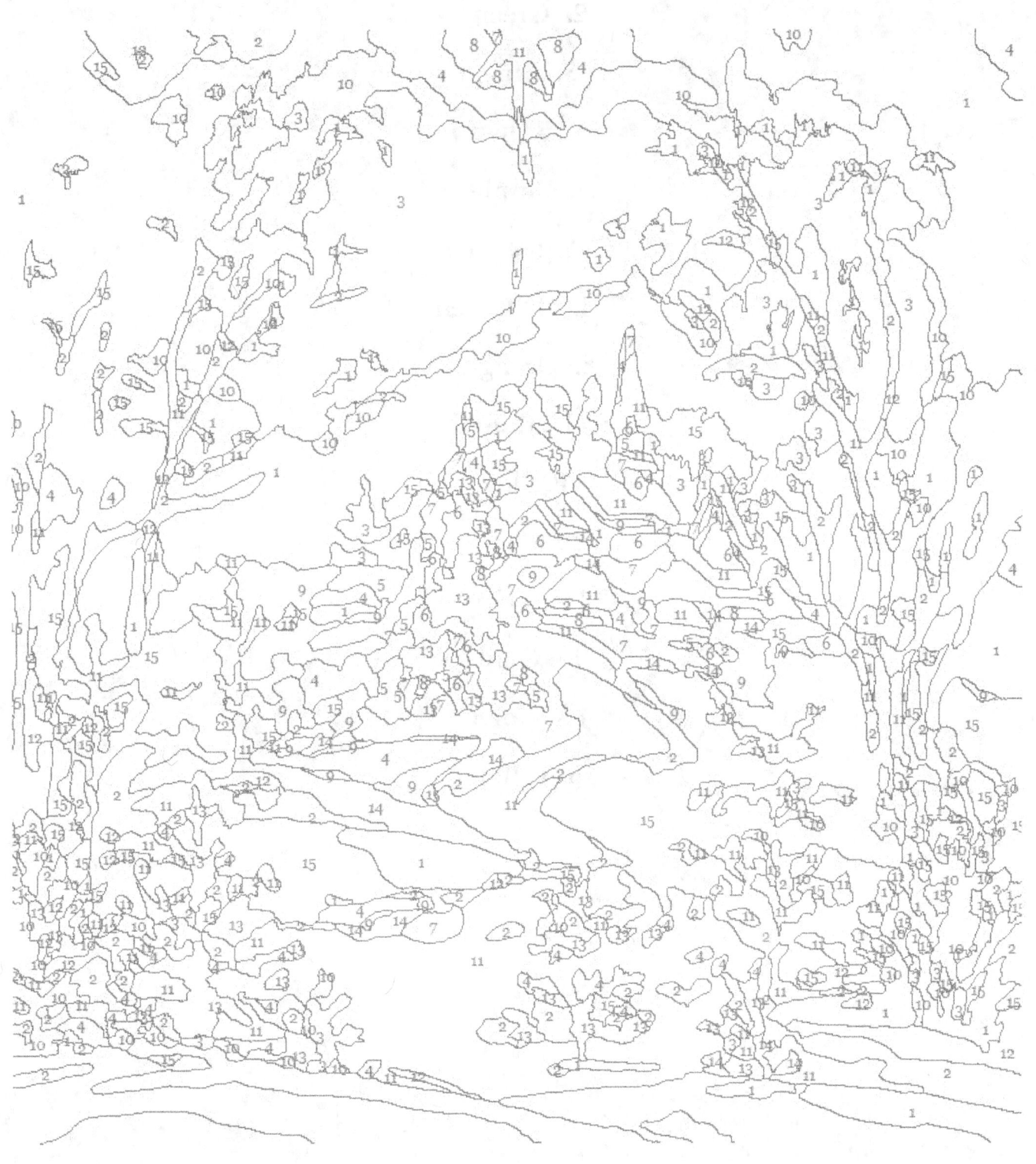

1. Red
2. Green
3. Blue
4. Brown
5. Purple
6. Light Blue
7. Light Green
8. Orange
9. Dark Red
10. Pink
11. Black
12. Dark Green
13. Gold
14. Violet
15. Yellow

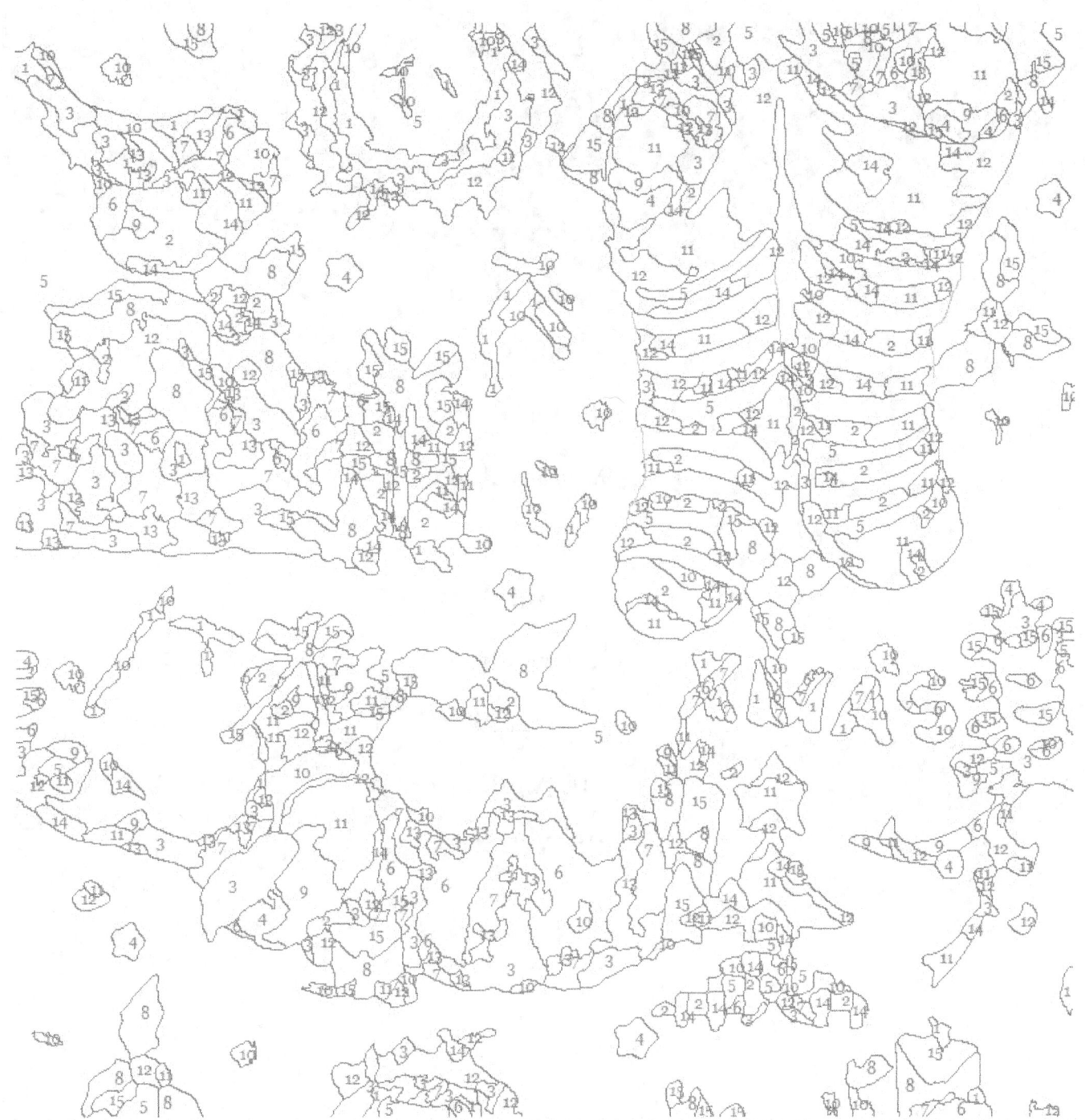

1. Red
2. Green
3. Blue
4. Brown
5. Purple
6. Light Blue
7. Light Green
8. Orange
9. Dark Red
10. Pink
11. Black
12. Dark Green
13. Gold
14. Violet
15. Yellow

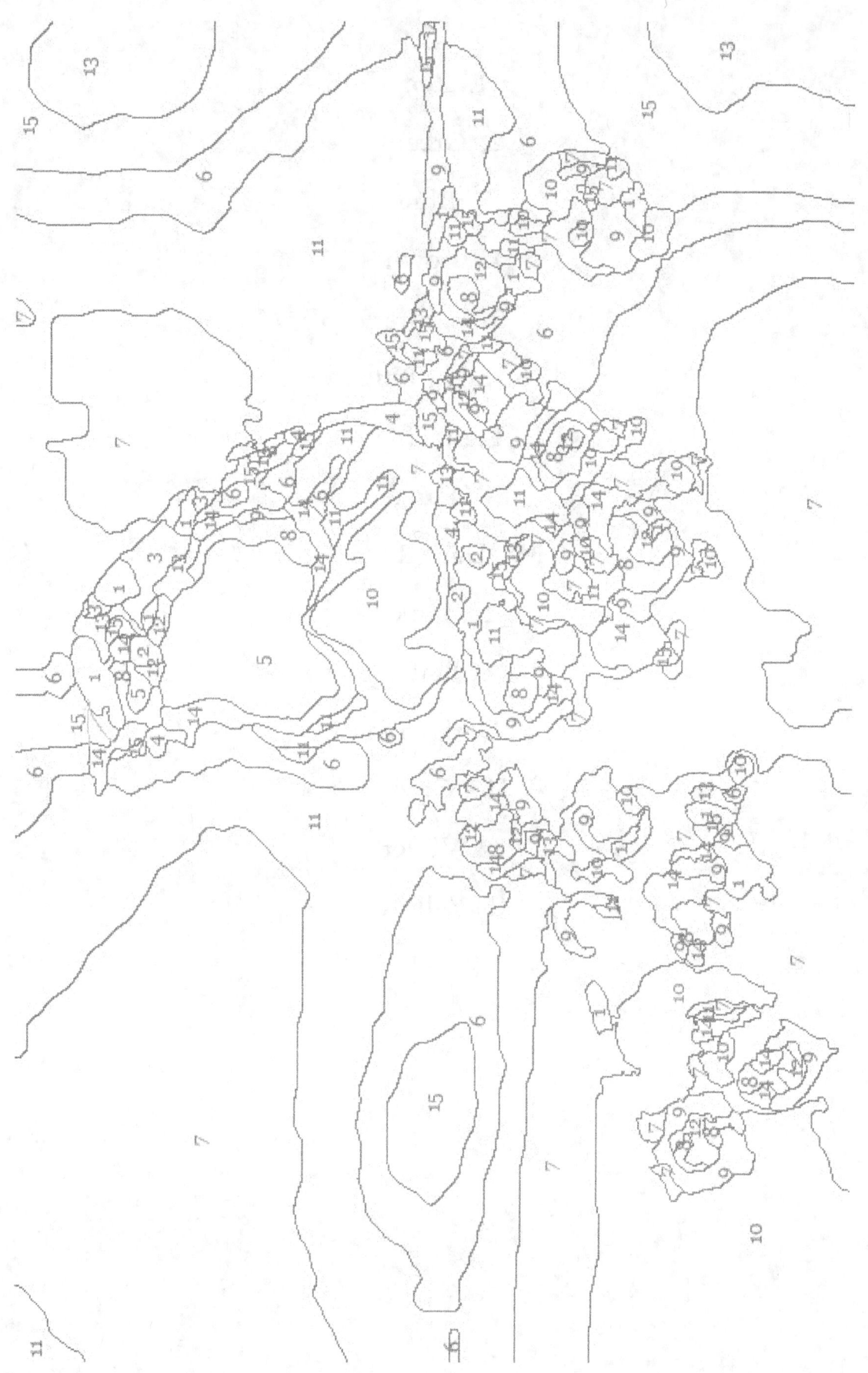

1. Red
2. Green
3. Blue
4. Brown
5. Purple
6. Light Blue
7. Light Green
8. Orange
9. Dark Red
10. Pink
11. Black
12. Dark Green
13. Gold
14. Violet
15. Yellow

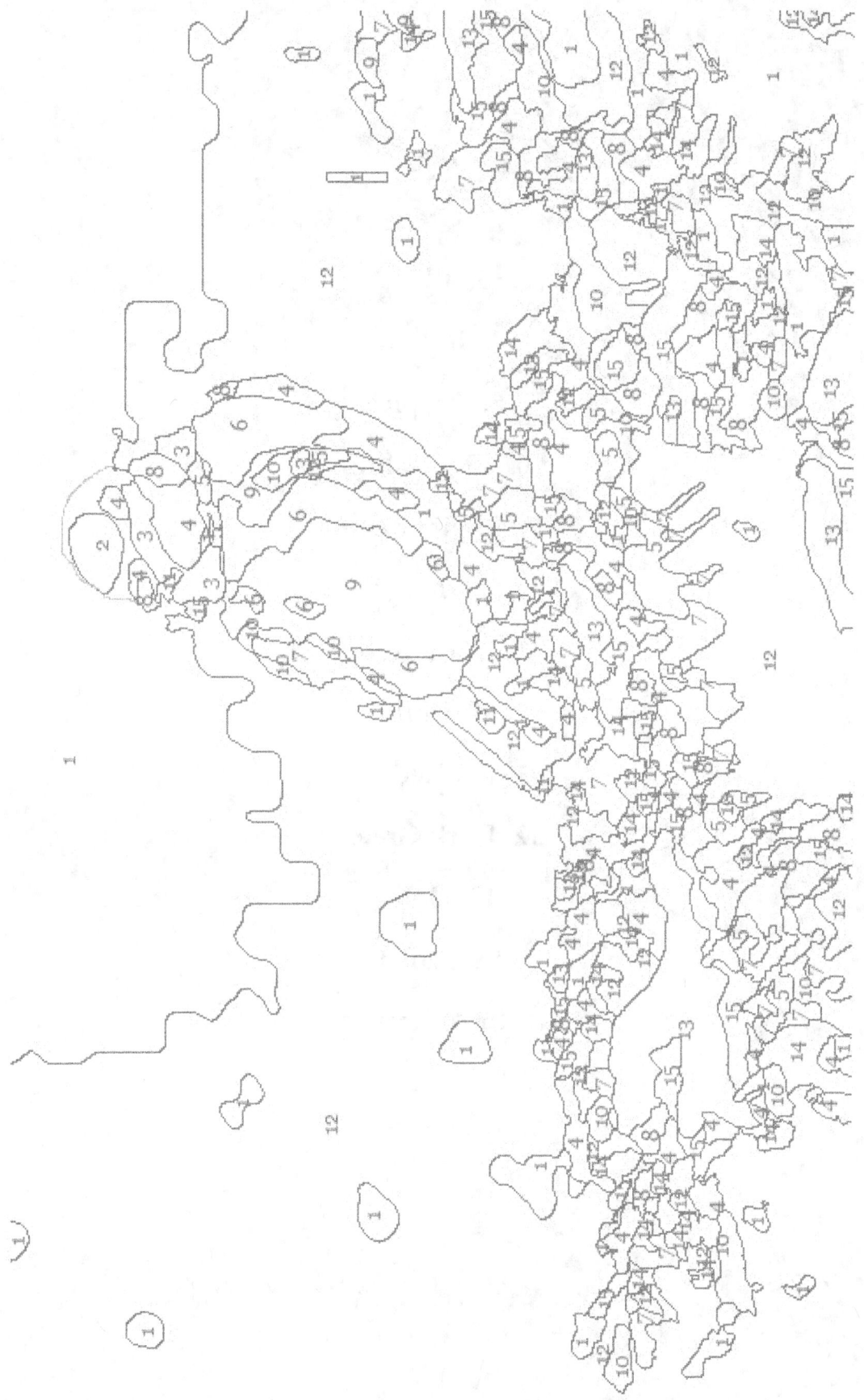

1. Black
2. Green
3. Blue
4. Brown
5. Purple
6. Light Blue
7. Light Green
8. Orange
9. Dark Red
10. Pink
11. Red
12. Dark Green
13. Gold
14. Violet
15. Yellow

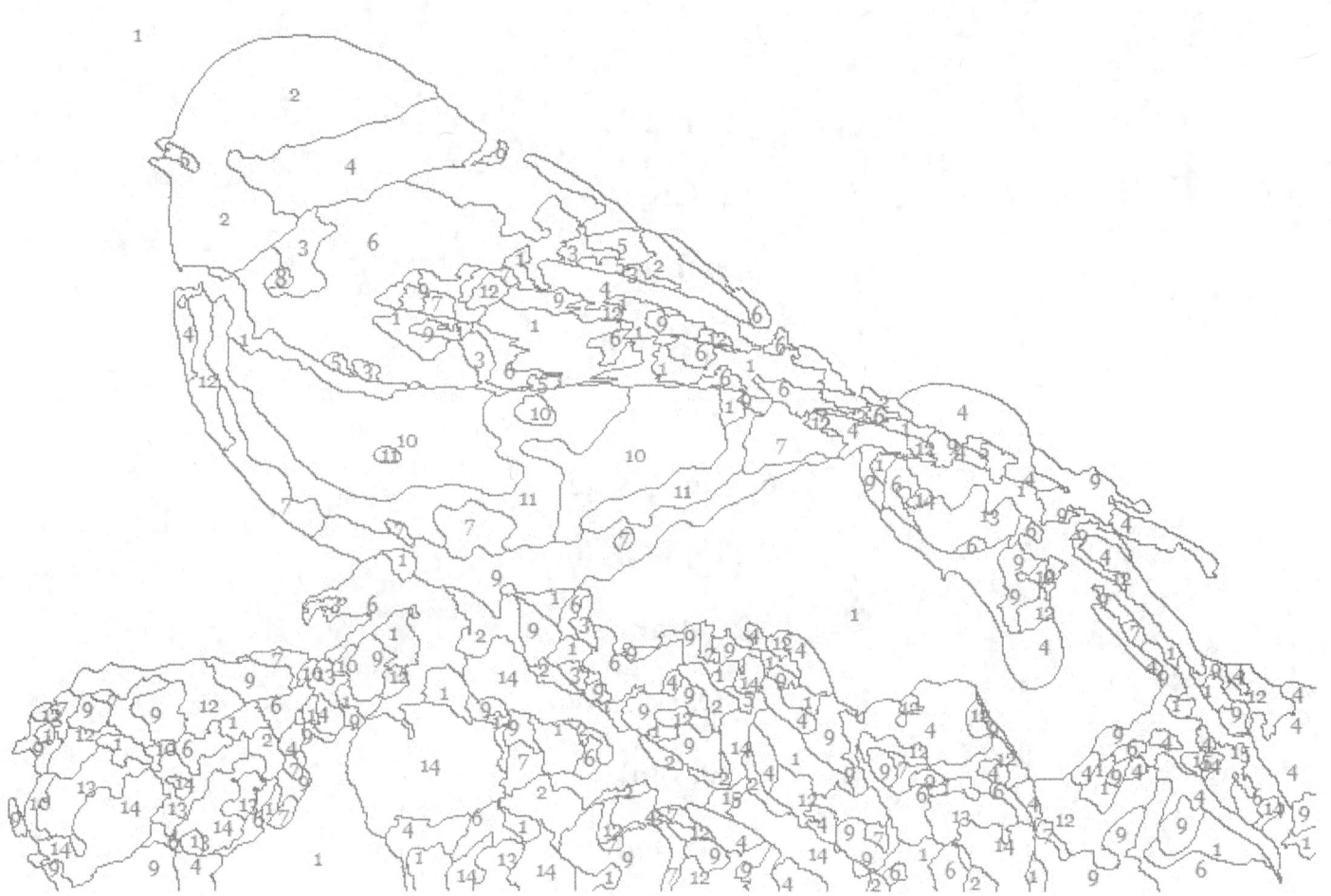

1. Black
2. Green
3. Blue
4. Brown
5. Purple
6. Light Blue
7. Light Green
8. Orange
9. Dark Red
10. Pink
11. Red
12. Dark Green
13. Gold
14. Violet
15. Yellow

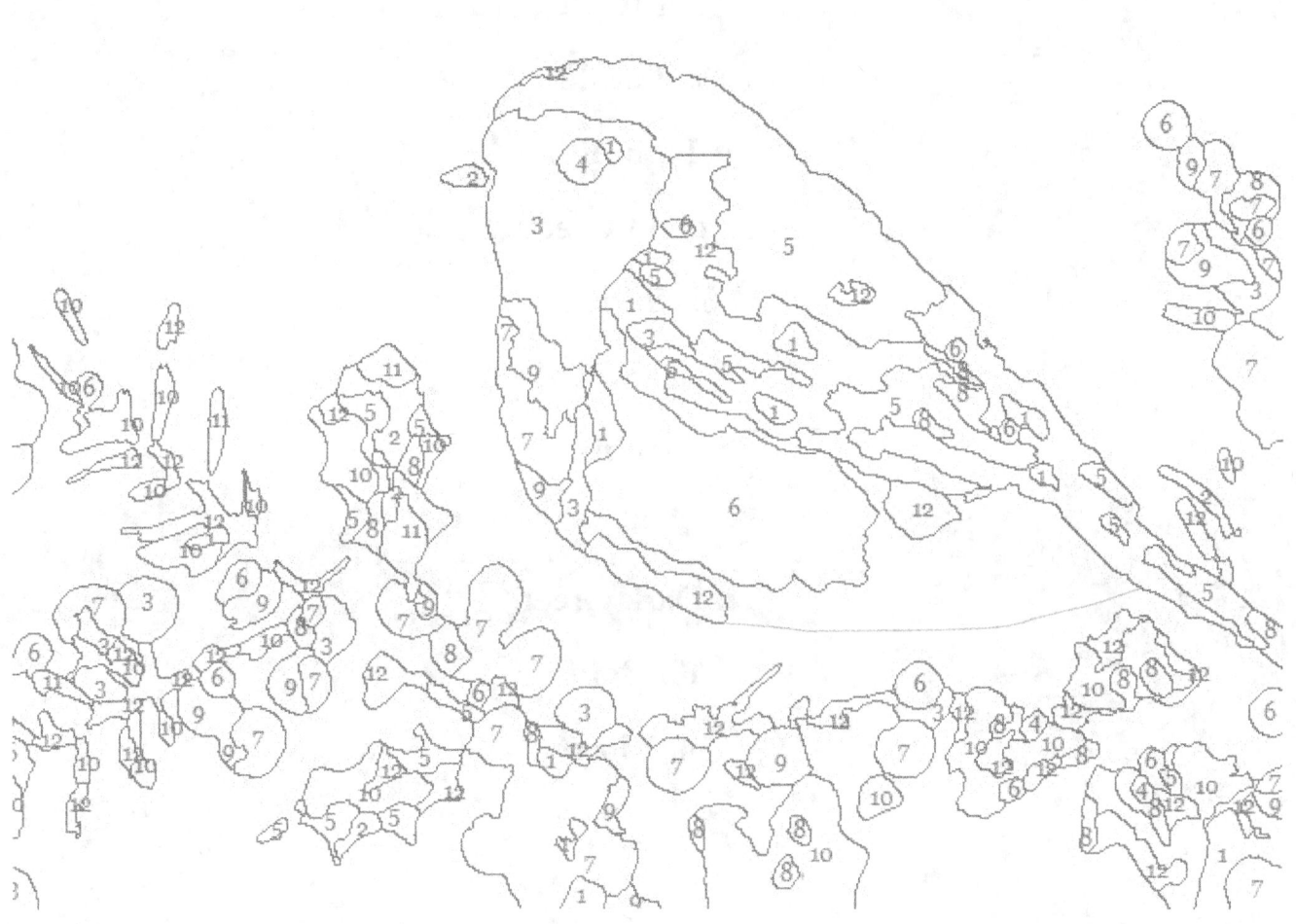

1. Black
2. Green
3. Blue
4. Brown
5. Purple
6. Light Blue
7. Light Green
8. Orange
9. Dark Red
10. Pink
11. Red
12. Dark Green
13. Gold
14. Violet
15. Yellow

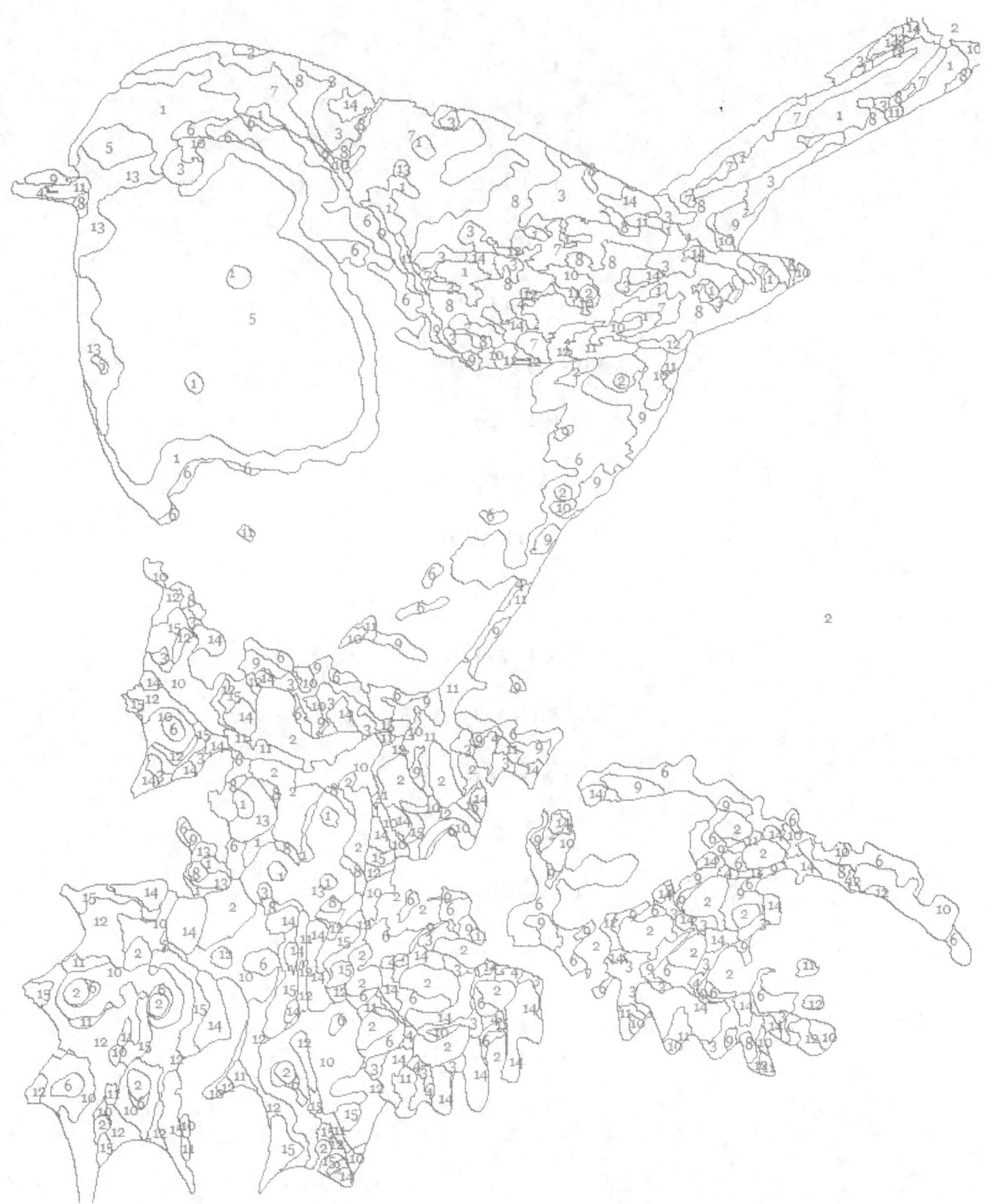

1. Red
2. Green
3. Blue
4. Brown
5. Purple
6. Light Blue
7. Light Green
8. Orange
9. Dark Red
10. Pink
11. Black
12. Dark Green
13. Gold
14. Violet
15. Yellow

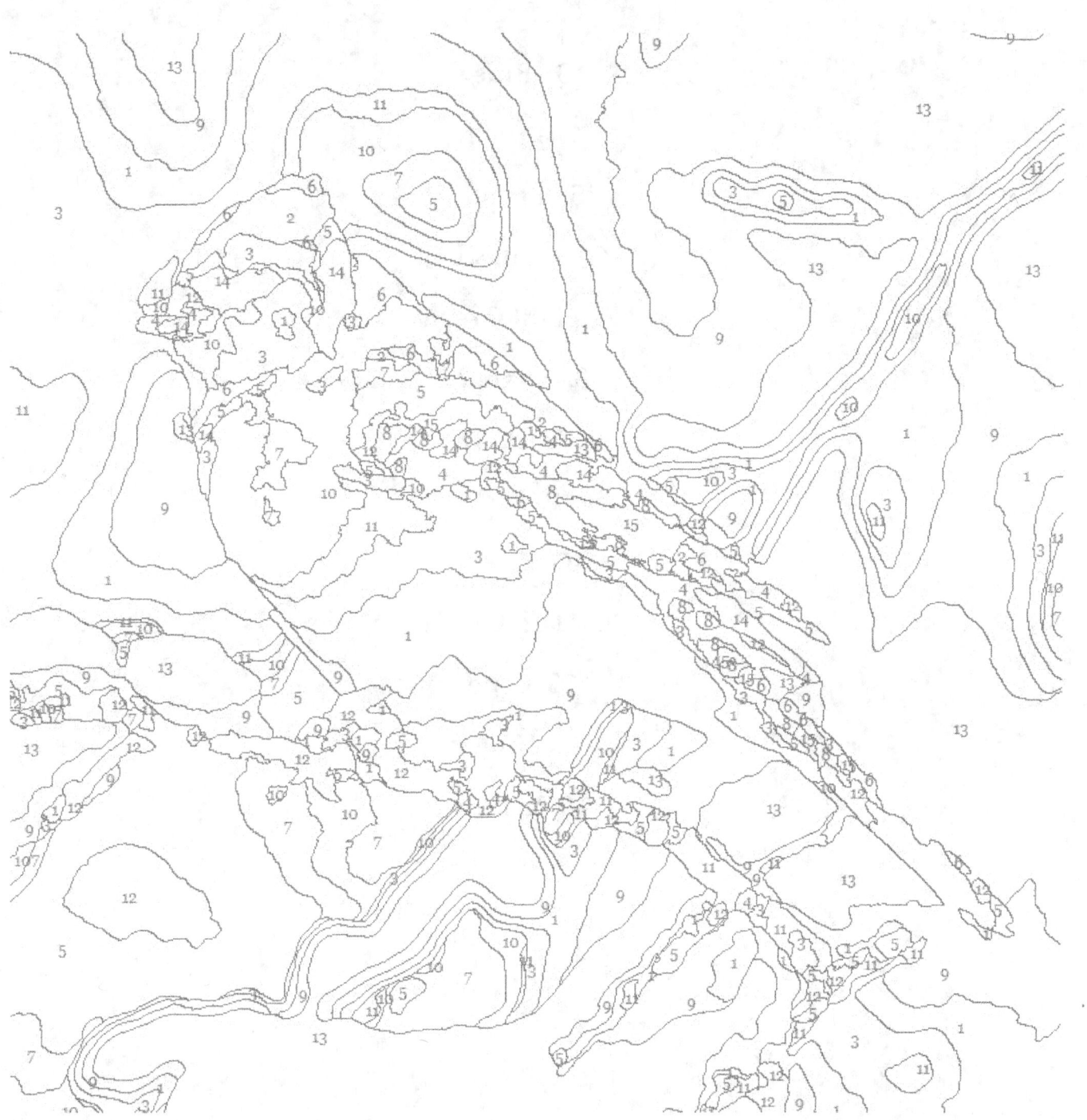

1. Red
2. Green
3. Blue
4. Brown
5. Purple
6. Light Blue
7. Light Green
8. Orange
9. Dark Red
10. Pink
11. Black
12. Dark Green
13. Gold
14. Violet
15. Yellow

Bonus Dot to Dot Christmas Puzzles

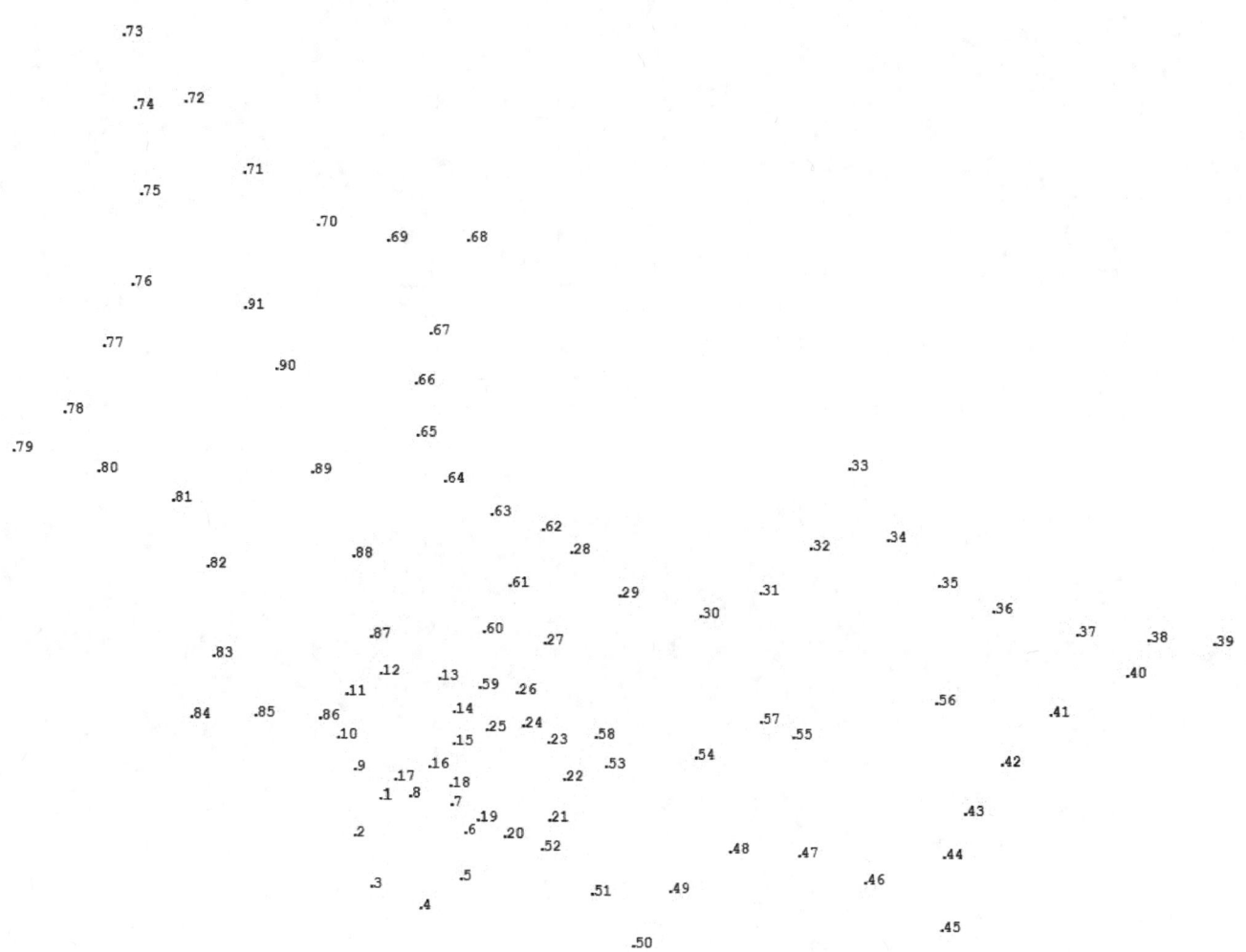

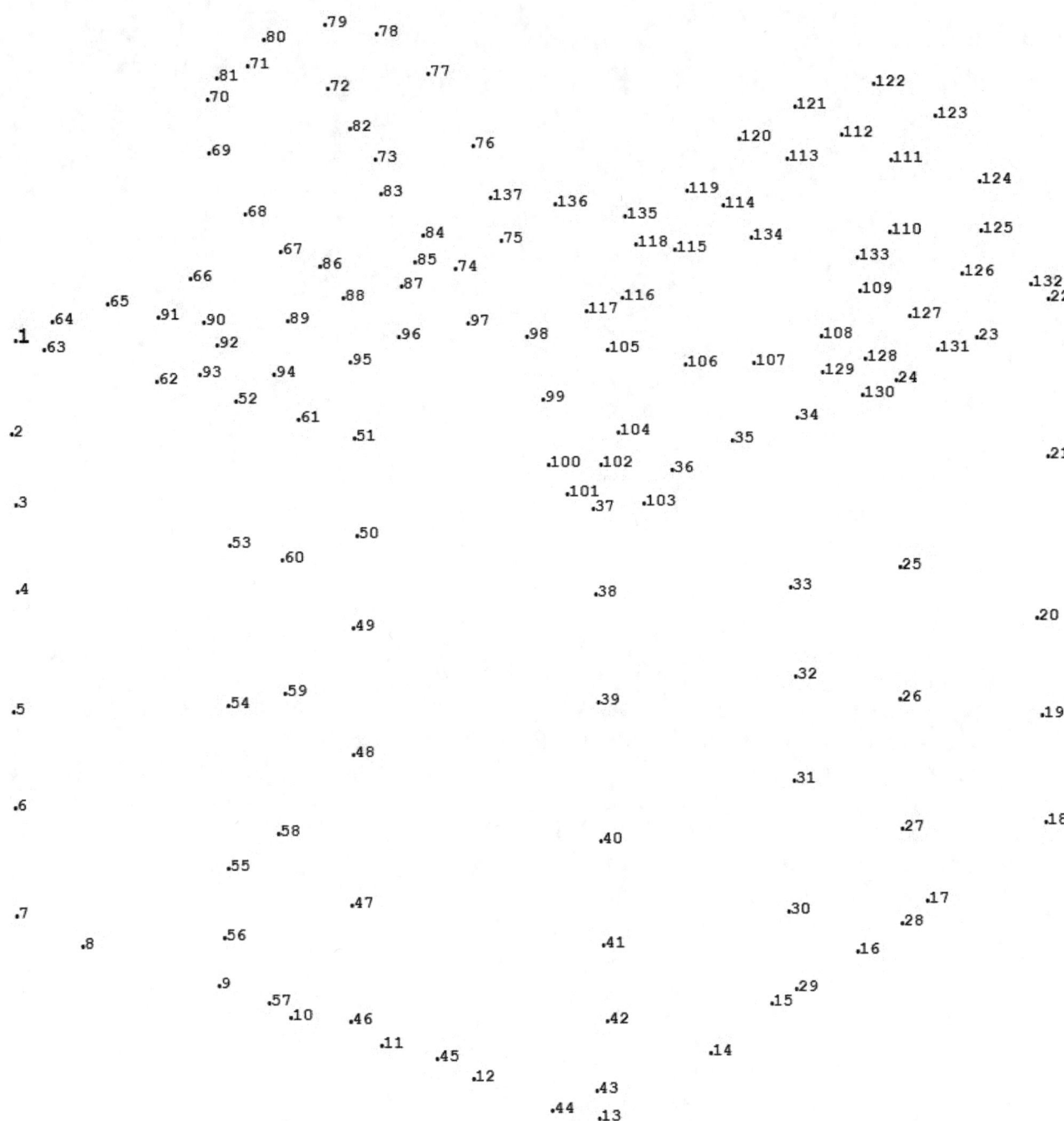

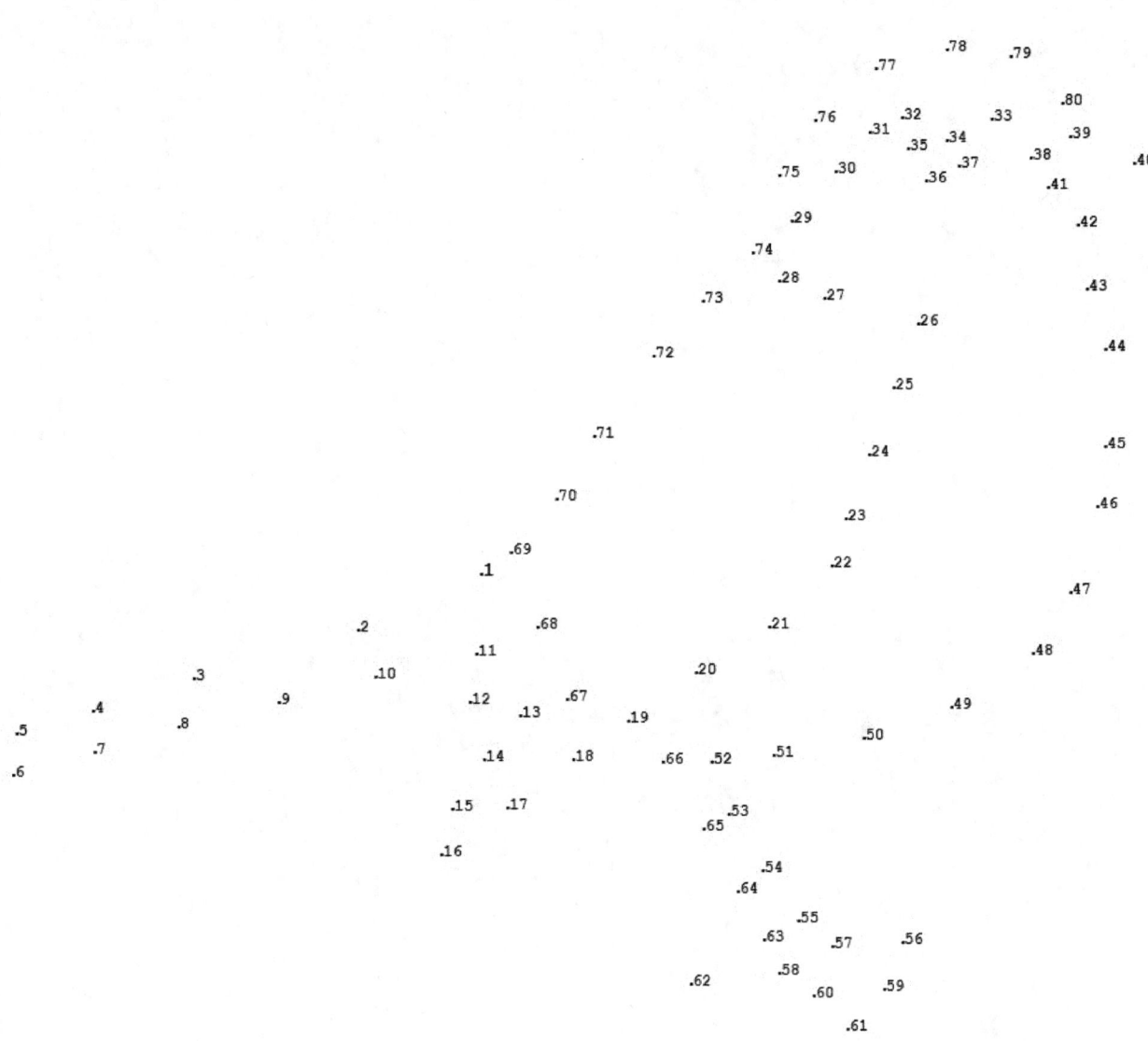

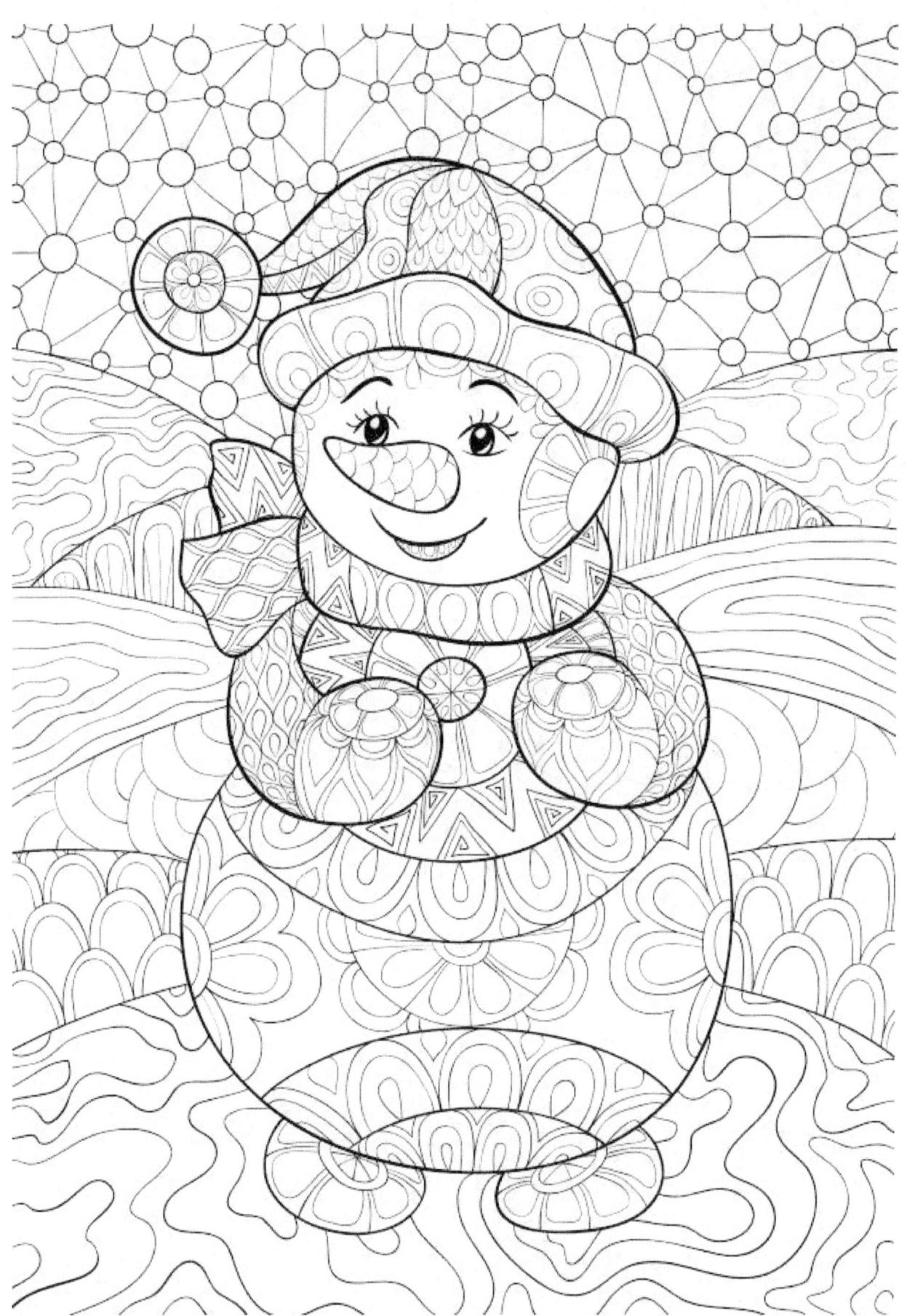

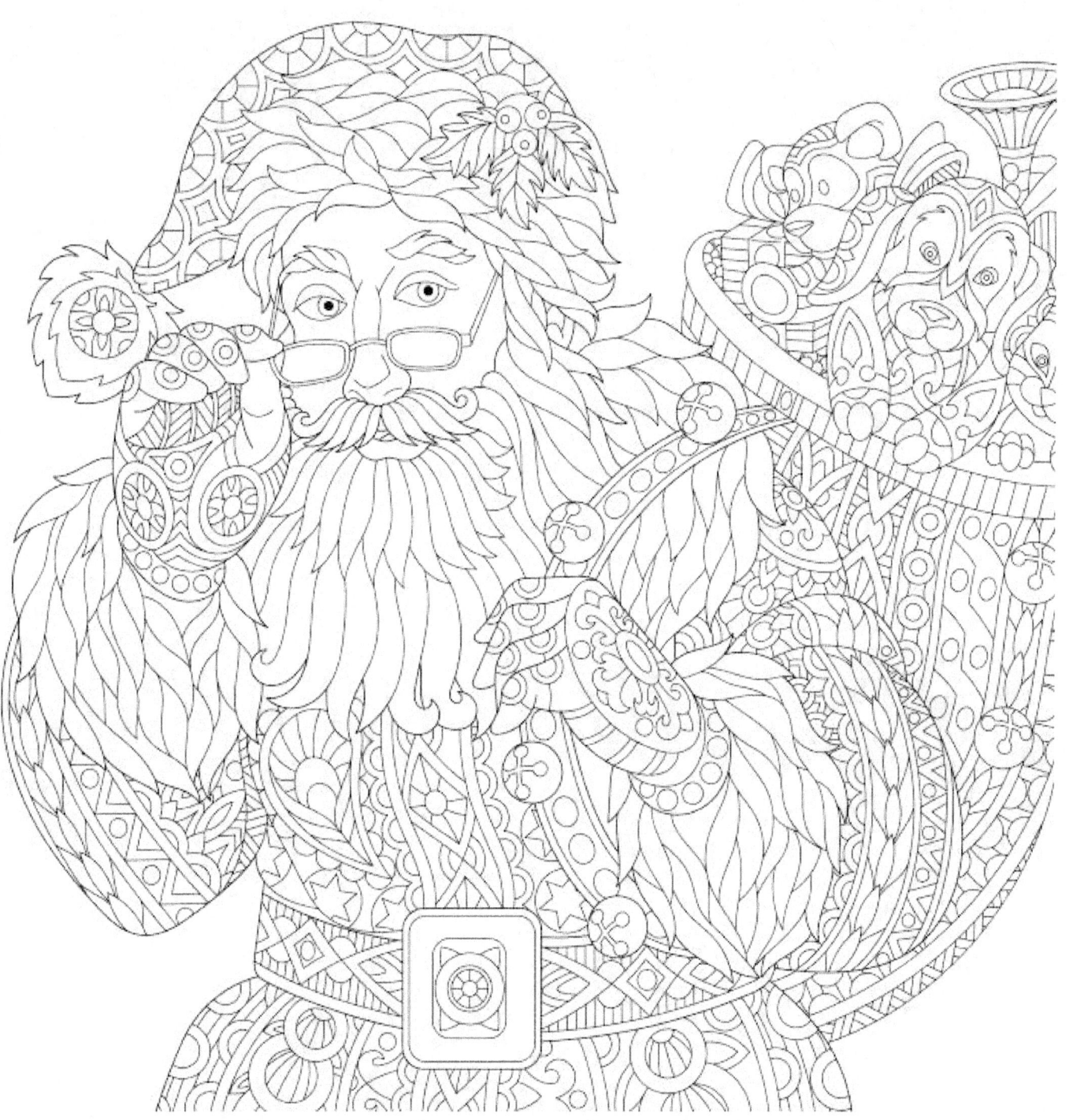

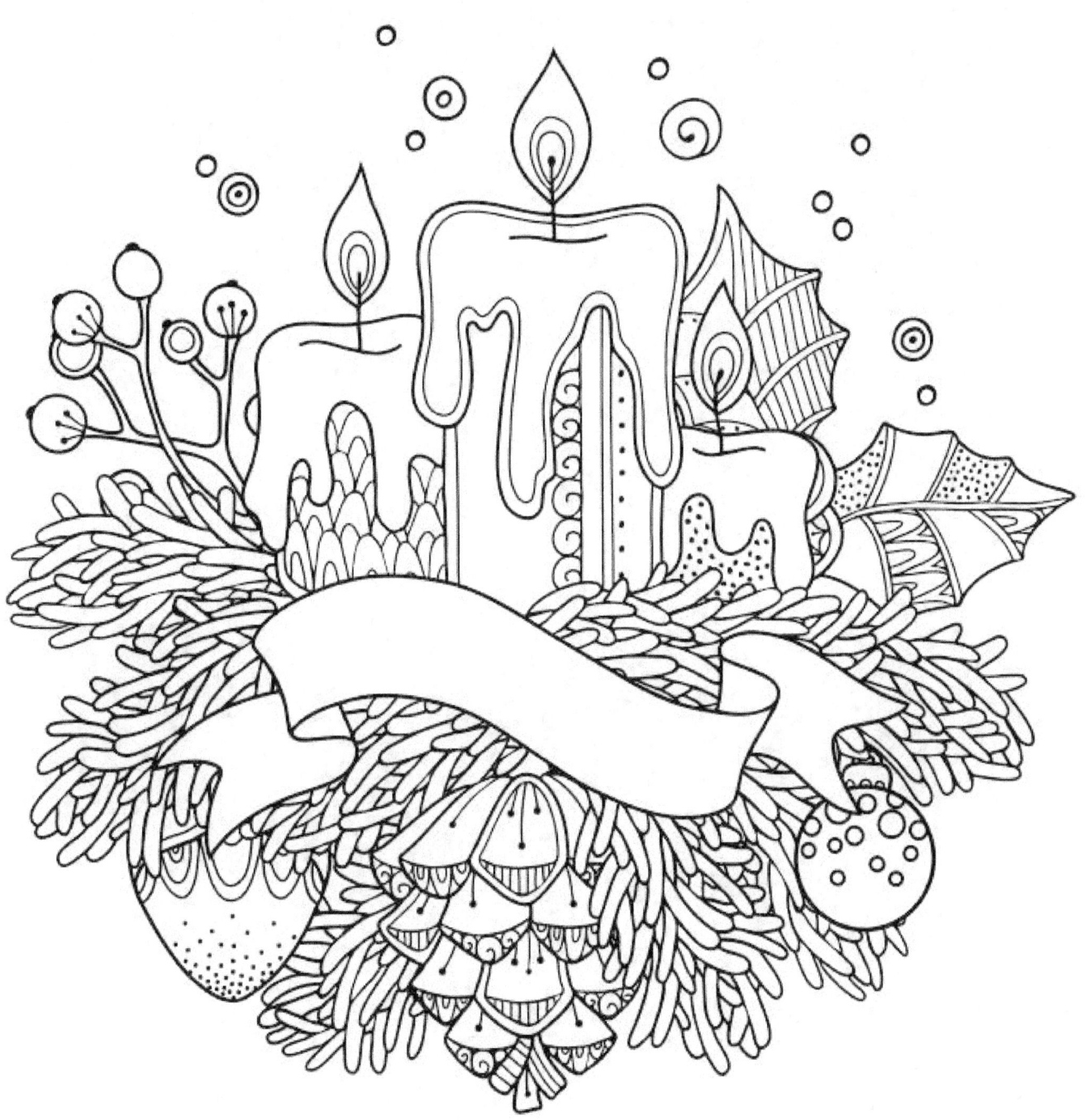

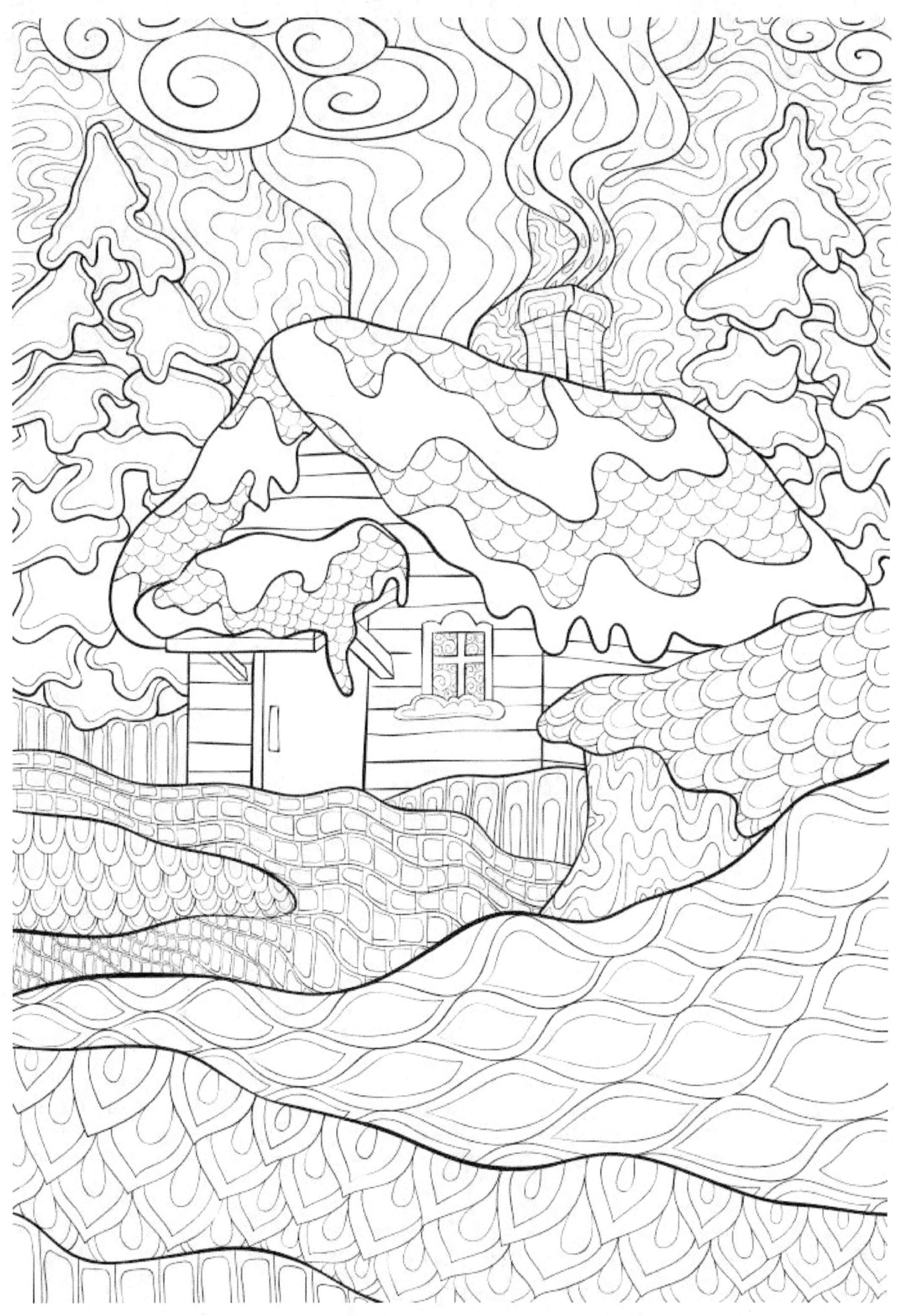

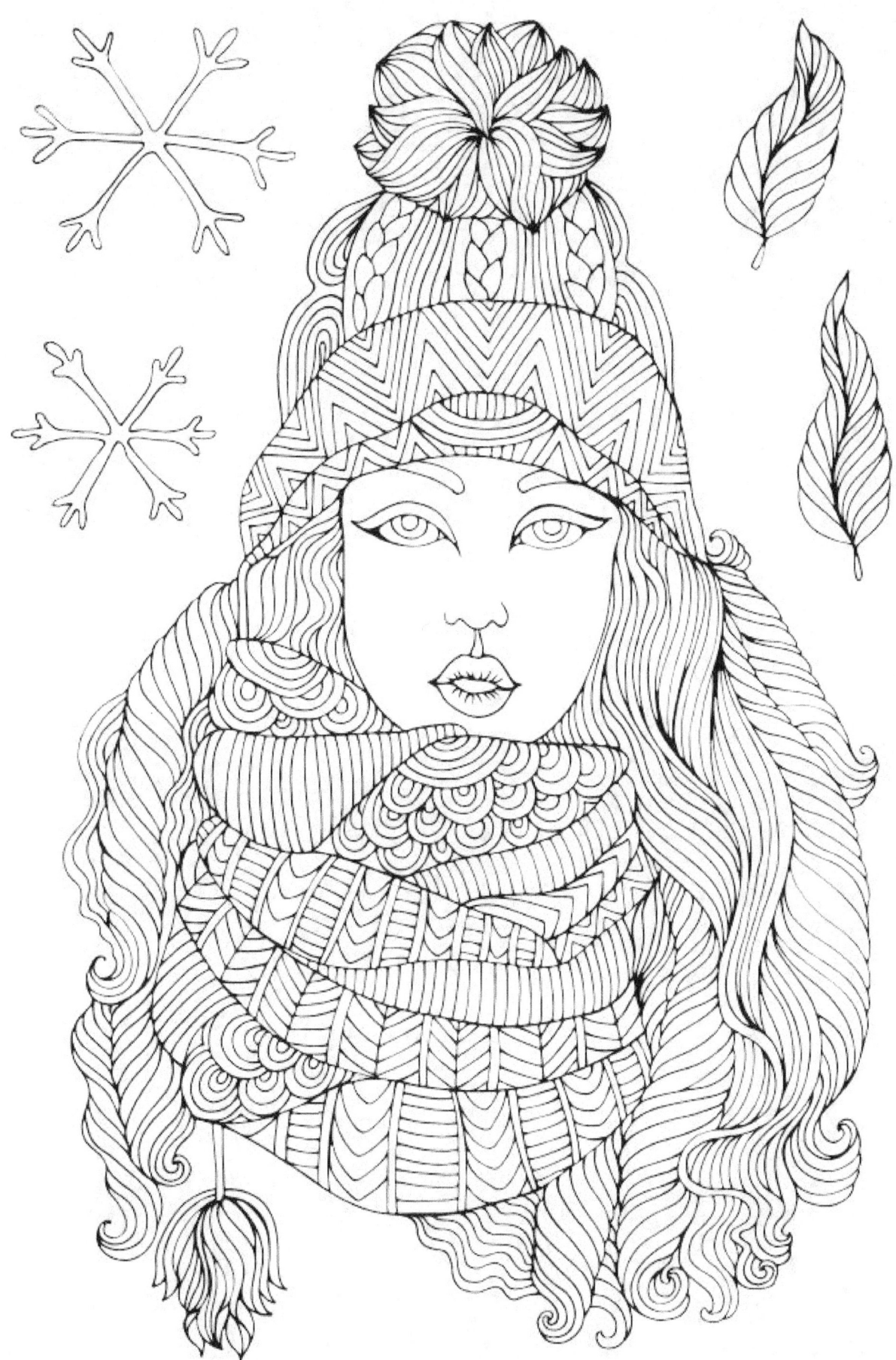